YOUR KNOWLEDGE HAS VALUE

- We will publish your bachelor's and master's thesis, essays and papers

- Your own eBook and book - sold worldwide in all relevant shops

- Earn money with each sale

Upload your text at www.GRIN.com and publish for free

Sexual Abuse in the Catholic Church. The Vicar of Christ, His Nemesis and a Prince's Scarlet Cardinal Sins

Tarcisius Mukuka

Bibliographic information published by the German National Library:

The German National Library lists this publication in the National Bibliography; detailed bibliographic data are available on the Internet at http://dnb.dnb.de.

ISBN: 9783346315359
This book is also available as an ebook.

Print and binding: Books on Demand GmbH, Norderstedt, Germany
Printed on acid-free paper from responsible sources.

The present work has been carefully prepared. Nevertheless, authors and publishers do not incur liability for the correctness of information, notes, links and advice as well as any printing errors.

GRIN web shop: https://www.grin.com/document/961955

Sexual Abuse in the Catholic Church Across the Big Pond
The Vicar of Christ, His Nemesis and a Prince's Cardinal Sins

By Dr Tarcisius Mukuka

Index

1. Introduction

This is the kind of analysis designed to bring one opprobrium and even episcopal dressing down that an unhappy former Catholic priest with a bone to chew with the One, Holy, Catholic and Apostolic Church is bringing ecclesiastical secrets into the open — a sort airing ecclesiastical dirty laundry in public. Following an earlier exchange with a prince of the Catholic Church responding to my *Facebook* post on the "Pope Francis supports same-sex unions"[1] brouhaha, a member of the Zambia Conference of Catholic Bishops, who shall remain unnamed out of respect for his office, chided me as follows, "It's not my intention to stop you from commenting on a number of issues concerning the Church. However, knowing you as someone who has formed many people in the Church and now teaches in other institutions of higher learning, a bit of restraint may be required of you so as not to distract the differently abled intellectuals who may not be as highly gifted as you are. Just my humble opinion [*Facebook* post, 24 October 2020]" (Mukuka 2020: 4). I was not sure how to take the "highly gifted as you are" remark. I took it as a compliment. I am not even sure what the point of "It's not my intention to stop you" was. It was never in his gift because I would be entitled to tell him to get on his episcopal bike or tell him where to stick his prohibition. And he was my former student to boot. So, first, I want to begin this article with a *caveat lector* [let the reader beware] and disclaimer. I do not intend to pull any punches and nothing I write here on the Catholic Church is not already in the open, especially with the recent publication of the "Report on the Holy See's institutional knowledge and decision-making related to former Cardinal Theodore Edgar McCarrick (1930 to 2017)," hereafter *McCarrick Report*, which is available on the Vatican Website.[2] At 449 pages long in its English version with 1409 footnotes [447 pages in Italian and 1410 footnotes], this is red meat to both liberal and conservative theological carnivores in the Catholic Church. Second, I am acting as no one's theological megaphone. The opinions are entirely mine. Third, I doff my hat to Papa Francesco for having refused the Carlo Maria Viganò bait when he accused him of harbouring a gay lobby in the Vatican and demanded his proverbial head on a platter when he called for him to resign. With the blessing of the ultra-conservative outlet, *LifeSite News*, he wrote "In this extremely dramatic moment for the universal Church, he must acknowledge his mistakes and, in keeping with the proclaimed principle of zero-tolerance, Pope Francis must be the first to set a good example for cardinals and bishops who covered up McCarrick's abuses and resign along with all of them."[3] At best, Carlo Maria Viganò was the kettle calling the pot black and at worst, simply duplicitous and wreaking of sour grapes for not getting the hoped for red biretta.

With Seraphic humility, Pope Francis deferred to the Vatican Secretariat of State to carry out a thorough two-year investigation and to author the report, "Published without waiver of privileges or immunities and with a full reservation of intellectual property and other rights." This article examines a triumvirate of relationships involving Pope Francis, Archbishop Carlo Maria Viganò and now defrocked former Cardinal Theodore Edgar McCarrick, relating to sexual abuse in the United States of America. Pope Francis' zero-tolerance was evident right from the beginning. As *Time* Magazine reported him saying, "On this issue we must go forward, forward. Zero tolerance," He told reporters as he returned from his trip to the Holy Land. He referred to abuse of children as an "ugly" crime that betrays God.[4] I will advance the

2

argument of this article as follows: Sexual abuse in the Catholic Church, a Pope from the ends of the earth with zero-tolerance for sexual abuse, a renegade papal diplomat with a bone to chew, a velvet prince and Lavender *Mafioso* of the Catholic Church, my initial shock upon reading the report and five takeaways from the *McCarrick Report* in that order. I argue that the *McCarrick Report* is a sign of a dysfunctional system held together by clericalism and patriarchy, secrecy and sovereignty. Sexual abuse in the Catholic Church will not be rooted out unless the two twin villains of clericalism and patriarchy, secrecy and sovereignty are thrown out of the tent. In terms of its hierarchy and how it is appointed, the process needs to reflect the rest of society, comprising male and female, straight and gay, married and celibate, young and old as well as being open, democratic and transparent.

2. Sexual Abuse in the Catholic Church

I am approaching the issue of sexual abuse in the Catholic Church as a human scourge as well as the product of a dysfunctional system propped by clericalism, patriarchy, secrecy and sovereignty. The problem is not reserved to the celibate Catholic priesthood. Research has shown that a higher percentage of sexual abuse occurs within families by celibates, non-celibates, heterosexuals and homosexuals, male and female, young and old. Sexual abuse is an equal opportunity employer which is not a respecter of persons. In the Catholic Church, it is largely a phenomenon of the Western Catholic Church held together by clericalism and patriarchy, secrecy and sovereignty as I have noted. In the African Catholic Church, our problem is sexual abuse of women, nuns and minors, usually teenage girls and on a smaller scale of homosexual sexual abuse of those in formation, especially in missionary-led institutions, with money covering a multitude of sins. In African society two forms of child abuse which includes sex are child marriages, child sex trafficking and neglect of children of ordained celibate priests, professed brothers and even bishops and archbishops.

2.1. What is the Issue?

In all this, the real scourge of sexual abuse is the vulnerability of children and abuse of power and trust. This was the tipping point for Pope Francis in the McCarrick case. As the *Child Rights International Network* [CRIN] points out, "Children have long suffered systemic sexual abuse within religious institutions all over the world — a centuries-old problem shrouded in secrecy, cover-ups, and a lack of accountability. The Catholic Church is one such institution which, in 2014, came under international scrutiny. The Holy See, the sovereign State headed by the Pope, who in turn heads the Roman Catholic Church, had its children's rights record reviewed by the United Nations for the first time in almost 20 years. The State was questioned primarily on the global scale of sexual abuse against children within the Church by its own clergy, the cover-ups that took place from the highest levels of authority, the denial of justice and compensation for victims, and the systemic failure to effectively protect children."[5]

In 2003, Bishop Accountability was set up. Among its objectives were: to document survivors' testimonies, provide links to networks supporting survivors, to track abusers on sexual offenders' registers, to document cover-ups etc.[6]

3

Regarding sexual abuse and the way that the Church has handled it in the past, the *McCarrick Report* is a first. As John Allen tells us, "for the most part, the report is searingly honest and comes off as a genuine attempt to get at the truth. It contains a level of detail never before seen. We're given the strictly confidential advice the most senior prelates in the Church gave when deciding to promote McCarrick, we're given the gut-wrenching details of victim testimony, and we're given first-hand recollections by top Vatican officials of the decision-making process. Such disclosure, on this scale, is absolutely new. The present power structure in the Vatican deserves credit not only for allowing this to happen, but for taking the heat as time wore on and impatience grew. We've been wondering for two years why it was taking so long, but seeing how thorough and painstakingly detailed the report is, that question no longer seems quite so pressing."[7] To vary a metaphor used in the conclusion of this article, now that the toothpaste is out of the tube, there is no putting it back in again.

2.2. What is the Problem?

The *Association of Rape Crisis Centres in Israel* (ARCCI), founded in 1990, describes sexual abuse as "an act of violence which the attacker uses against someone they perceive as weaker than them. It does not come from an uncontrollable sex drive, but is a crime committed deliberately with the goal of controlling and humiliating the victim."[8] Sexual abuse is a symptom of an illness such as alcoholism. This does not mean, it is uncontrollable. People who abuse in clerical collar would have abused without the benefit of the Roman collar. Celibacy did not lead them to abuse. It facilitated and nurtured their illness as will become clear in the case of Theodore McCarrick. In fact, what exacerbated their illness is a clerical and patriarchal culture of which the Catholic Church is the quintessential exemplar bar none. In the case of the Vatican, this was exacerbated by secrecy and sovereignty, thanks to the 1929 Lateran Treaty. Child sexual abuse [CSA], also called child molestation, is a form of abuse in which an adult or older adolescent uses a child for sexual stimulation and self-satisfaction. Forms of child sexual abuse include engaging in sexual activities with a child, whether by asking or pressuring, or by other means, indecent exposure of the genitals, female nipples, etc., sexting, child grooming, and child sexual exploitation, including using a child to produce child pornography.

Child sexual abuse can occur in a variety of settings: home, school, Church, episcopal palace or workplace (in the case of child labour). In Africa, child marriage is one of the main forms of child sexual abuse. UNICEF has stated that child marriage "represents perhaps the most prevalent form of sexual abuse and exploitation of girls."[9] The effects of child sexual abuse include physical injury, depression, anxiety, sleep disorders, complex post-traumatic stress disorder, propensity to further victimisation in adulthood, among other problems. Sexual abuse by a family member in the form of incest can result in more serious and long-term psychological trauma, especially in the case of parental incest. This is a vicious circle. People who are abused in childhood often end up abusers as adults. In a 1989 *New York Times* report, Daniel Goleman concluded that "Studies also now indicate that about one-third of people who are abused in childhood will become abusers themselves. This is a lower percentage than many experts had expected, but obviously poses a major social challenge. The research also confirms that abuse in childhood increases the likelihood in adulthood of problems ranging from depression and alcoholism to sexual maladjustment and multiple personality."[10]

4

A 2009 study of the global prevalence of child sexual abuse put it at 19.7% for females and 7.9% for males (Pereda *et al* 2009: 328–338). I take this to mean those who suffer. Most sexual abuse offenders were acquainted with their victims; approximately 30% were relatives of the child, most often brothers, fathers, uncles, or cousins. Theodore McCarrick referred to them as "nephews and nieces." Around 60% were other acquaintances, such as friends of the family, babysitters, or neighbours. Strangers were offenders in approximately 10% of child sexual abuse cases. Most child sexual abuse was committed by men. Studies on female child molesters show that women commit 14% to 40% of offenses reported against boys and 6% of offenses reported against girls.[11] According to the Jesuit priest, James Martin, an advocate for gay rights in the Catholic Church, "Around the same time as the *National Review Board* released their findings, the John Jay College of Criminal Justice concluded a nationwide study, reporting that around four percent of American priests between 1950 and 2002 had been accused of abuse."[12]

2.3. What is the Solution?

I am jumping the gun here but in the Catholic Church, three solutions may help to address sexual abuse of children: complete transparency, not *post factum* but when the delict is committed, jettisoning clericalism and patriarchy, better accompaniment and discernment for vocations to the priesthood and religious life and better vetting and open election of bishops by their constituents with a limited term or terms or a much lower age of retirement than the current geriatric 75. As CRIN pointed out, "To begin improving its appalling children's rights record, the UN recommended that the Holy See reform the Church's internal procedures, namely in the areas of child protection and abuse prevention, transparency and reporting, and accountability. But obscure and rigid internal structures and a chronic lack of political will continue to delay any progress. These factors inevitably pave the way for some of the worst crimes against children to continue and for survivors to be denied justice."[13]

3. A Pope from the Ends of the Earth with Zero-Tolerance for Sexual Abuse

On a drizzly 13 March 2013 Rome evening, a hitherto little-known Argentinian Cardinal of Italian origin, Jorge Mario Bergoglio, introduced himself to the city and to the world — *Urbi et Orbi* — "Brothers and sisters, good evening! You all know that the duty of the Conclave was to give Rome a bishop. It seems that my brother cardinals have gone almost to the ends of the earth to get him [*Fratelli e sorelle, buonasera! Voi sapete che il dovere del Conclave era di dare un vescovo a Roma. Sembra che i miei fratelli cardinali siano andati a prenderlo quasi alla fine del mondo*].[14] Already the name Papa Francesco was gaining currency. On that evening, he thanked his audience and asked them to pray for his predecessor, Benedict XVI. He led the audience in saying the *Our Father*, *Hail Mary* and *Glory Be*. The tone was pastoral and compassionate, like a new parish priest assuring his new parishioners that we were going to get along famously. "And now, let's begin this journey: bishop and people. This journey of the Church of Rome, which presides in charity over the other Churches. A journey of fraternity, love and trust between us. Pray for us: one for the other. Let's pray for all the world, so that it may be a grand fraternity. I hope that this journey of the Church, which we begin today and in which my Cardinal Vicar present here will help me that it may be fruitful for the evangelisation of this beautiful city" [*E adesso, incominciamo questo cammino: Vescovo e popolo. Questo cammino della Chiesa di Roma, che è quella che presiede nella carità tutte le Chiese. Un cammino di fratellanza, di amore, di fiducia tra noi. Preghiamo sempre per noi: l'uno per l'altro. Preghiamo per tutto il mondo, perché ci sia una grande fratellanza. Vi auguro che questo cammino di Chiesa, che oggi incominciamo e nel quale mi aiuterà il mio Cardinale Vicario, qui presente, sia fruttuoso per l'evangelizzazione di questa città tanto bella!*][15]

From what we can tell from his immediate pronouncements and appointments, there were at least three items in his in-tray: sexual abuse in the Catholic Church, especially sexual abuse of minors, financial mismanagement or financial reform and homosexuality in the Church. We focus here on the first item. In December 2013, Cardinal Sean O'Malley, the Archbishop of Boston, announced that Pope Francis was setting up a panel of experts to provide codes of conduct for clergymen, guidelines for Church officials and better checks for would-be priests on the issue of sexual abuse. "Up until now there has been so much focus on the judicial parts of this but the pastoral part is very, very important. The Holy Father is concerned about that," he said. "We feel that having the advantage of a commission of experts who will be able to study these issues and bring concrete recommendations for the Holy Father and the Holy See will be very important."[16] That was then. 7 years later, Pope Francis is still intent on applying zero-tolerance to sexual abuse in the Catholic Church. On 11 November 2020, Nicole Winfield reported that "Pope Francis pledged Wednesday to rid the Catholic Church of sexual abuse and offered prayers to victims of former Cardinal Theodore McCarrick, a day after the Vatican released a detailed report into the decades long Church cover-up of his sexual misconduct."[17] Nicole Winfield let us into one of the shocks of the recent report, "The Vatican report blamed a host of bishops, cardinals and Popes for downplaying and dismissing mountains of evidence of McCarrick's misconduct starting in the 1990s — but largely spared Francis. Instead, it laid the lion's share of the blame on St. John Paul II, a former Pope, for having appointed McCarrick archbishop of Washington in 2000, and making him a cardinal, despite having commissioned an inquiry that found he had slept with seminarians."[18]

But as the *McCarrick Report* notes, "On 6 October 2018, the Holy Father ordered a thorough study of the documentation present in the Archives of the Dicasteries and Offices of the Holy See regarding McCarrick, in order to ascertain all the relevant facts, to place them in their historical context and to evaluate them objectively" (*McCarrick Report* 2020: 1). The report has been in the making for the last 2 years. Sceptics are unlikely to be convinced by the Secretariat of State's disclaimer that "the examination did not reveal evidence that McCarrick's customary gift-giving and donations impacted significant decisions made by the Holy See regarding McCarrick during any period" (*McCarrick Report* 2020: 4). Money is a universal language and Theodore McCarrick, or as he liked to be referred to by his "nephews and nieces," Uncle Ted, appears to have used it cunningly.

By the time of his election, Pope Francis already knew of Theodore McCarrick. In fact, while Archbishop of Buenos Aires, he met him on 17 December 2004, on his birthday. Once Pope Francis got to hear of sexual abuse allegations against Theodore McCarrick, especially relating to minors, he was quick to move in with a zero-tolerance sledge hammer. "In June 2017, the Archdiocese of New York learned of the first known allegation of sexual abuse by McCarrick of a victim under 18 years of age, which occurred in the early 1970s. Shortly after the accusation was deemed credible, Pope Francis requested McCarrick's resignation from the College of Cardinals. Following an administrative penal process by the *Congregation for the Doctrine of the Faith*, McCarrick was found culpable of acts in contravention of the Sixth Commandment of the Decalogue involving both minors and adults, and on that basis was dismissed from the clerical state" (*McCarrick Report* 2020: 14). That, as I have noted, was Pope Francis' tipping point. It mattered little that Theodore McCarrick was an octogenarian. He never worried about the age of his victims, why should the Church worry about his? Not surprisingly, the whereabouts of the disgraced former high-flying prince of the Catholic Church are unknown. According to the *National Catholic Reporter*, his last known residence was "St. Fidelis Friary, run by the Capuchin Franciscan order in Victoria, Kansas, in the Diocese of Salina in the north-western part of the state."[19]

4. A Renegade Papal Diplomat with a bone to chew

Apart from Theodore McCarrick, the other *bête noire* of the report into the sexual misdemeanours of the former Cardinal of Washington is the former Vatican ambassador to the USA, Carlo Maria Viganò. Born in northern Italy with a silver spoon in his mouth, he was ordained a priest in 1968. Five years later, he entered the Vatican's diplomatic corps, where he held positions at embassies in Great Britain and Iraq. He worked more than a decade (1978–1989) in the Vatican Secretariat of State before spending the next three years as the Vatican's permanent observer mission at the Council of Europe, in Strasbourg, France. He was made an archbishop in 1992 by Pope John Paul II, who appointed him Apostolic Nuncio to Nigeria. For much of his early years in Rome, he kept a low profile, working mostly behind the scenes, dotting all the I's and crossing all the T's necessary for rising on the ladder of a career diplomatic.

That low profile extended into his appointment in 2009 to a high-ranking position as secretary-general of the governorate of Vatican City State. There he earned a reputation for his skills as a financial reformer. He also faced internal tensions and criticism for what some viewed as micromanaging. In 2010, anonymous emails circulated among cardinals and Vatican embassies alleging nepotism by Carlo Maria Viganò in the career of his nephew, Msgr. Carlo Maria Polvani, who also worked within the Vatican Secretariat of State. A commentary in the Italian newspaper *Il Giornale*, also anonymous, suggested he sought control over Vatican security services.

Despite writing to Pope Benedict XVI requesting to keep his Vatican position, Carlo Maria Viganò was appointed on 19 October 2011, as Apostolic *Nuncio* to the USA, succeeding Archbishop Pietro Sambi, who died earlier that year. The move was seen as a spanner in the works of his hopes of eventually being appointed president of the Vatican City State and with it, elevation to a Cardinal's office in the model of a latter-day Paul Marcinkus. The rest of Carlo Maria Viganò's comportment in relation to Pope Francis can be expressed by this sour grapes' incident even though Francis was nowhere near his appointments to and recall from the USA. Since his return from Washington without any sign or hope for the hoped-for red hat, he has been pouring vitriol on Pope Francis and peddling one conspiracy after another which included blaming Pope Francis for the McCarrick sexual abuse scandal.[20] This included accusing Pope Francis of sheltering a gay lobby in the Vatican. Pope Francis refused to take the bait. With the *McCarrick Report*, Pope Francis can now return the favour. But by no means, is Pope Francis off the hook. Given what he knew or found in his in-tray about Theodore McCarrick, he had no right to trust the judgement of his two immediate predecessors.

On 20 October 2020, Carlo Maria Viganò wrote on Marco Tosatti's ultra conservative website, *Stilum Curiae*, "After all, experience teaches us that when Bergoglio says something, he does it with a very precise purpose: to make others interpret his words in the broadest possible sense. The front pages of newspapers all over the world are announcing today: 'The Pope approves Gay Marriage' — even if technically this is not what he said. But this was exactly the result that he and the Vatican gay lobby wanted. Then the Vatican Press Office will perhaps say that what Bergoglio said was misunderstood, that this was an old interview, and that the Church reaffirms its condemnation of homosexuality as intrinsically disordered. But the damage has been done, and even any steps backwards from the scandal that has been stirred up will ultimately be a step forward in the direction of mainstream thought and what is politically correct. Let us not forget the nefarious results of his famous utterance in 2013 — 'Who am I to judge?' — which earned him a place on the cover of *The Advocate* along with the title 'Man of the Year.'"[21]

On 25 August 2018, Carlo Maria Viganò published an 11-page letter accusing Pope Francis and numerous other senior Church leaders of concealing allegations of sexual misconduct against then-cardinal Theodore McCarrick. After the publication of the letter, he continued to issue public statements critical of Pope Francis. With the recent publication of the "Report on the Holy See's institutional knowledge and decision-making related to former Cardinal Theodore Edgar McCarrick (1930 to 2017)," the former Church diplomat may have handed Pope Francis the final nail in Carlo Maria Viganò's coffin. To his credit, while serving in the Secretariat of State, Carlo Maria Viganò wrote two *memoranda*, one in 2006 and the other in 2008, raising questions about Theodore McCarrick. The *memoranda* referenced allegations and rumours about Theodore McCarrick's misconduct during the 1980s. He noted that the allegations remained unproven, "*Si vera et probata sunt exposita*" [if what is asserted be true and proven] and that only the Pope could judge a cardinal under canon law. He suggested that a canonical process could be opened to determine the truth and, if warranted, to impose an "exemplary measure" (*McCarrick Report* 2020: 10). But it seems these concerns, having found their way into Pope Benedict's in-tray never left the pending tray until now.

Once *nuncio* in the USA, Carlo Maria Viganò, the papal ambassador was presented with Priest 3's lawsuit which alleged that overt sexual conduct between him and Theodore McCarrick had occurred in 1991. But as the *McCarrick Report* notes, Carlo Maria Viganò "did not take these steps and therefore never placed himself in the position to ascertain the credibility of Priest 3" (*McCarrick Report* 2020: 12). Carlo Maria Viganò's involvement in the McCarrick case went back to 6 December 2006 — at that time he was Delegate for Pontifical Representations within the Secretariat of State — when he wrote a memorandum on "Card. Theodore McCarrick: Allegations of Homosexuality" (*McCarrick Report* 2020: 262–265). After reading the lengthy and detailed memorandum, Archbishop Leonardo Sandri, Substitute of the Secretariat of State, signed on the memorandum with the following words, *"Si vera sunt exposita"* [if what is asserted be true and proven]: The least one can imagine would be a prohibition against any public pastoral activity, guiding him towards a retired life of penance and prayer. But would that be sufficient?" (*McCarrick Report* 2020: 265). Clearly, this was not and more was to come.

Archbishop Carlo Maria Viganò followed up with another memorandum in 2008, in similar vein as the 2006 memorandum. And to be fair to Carlo Maria Viganò, he ended this second memorandum with the clear recommendation that "The case of Card. McCarrick, as has been said, is within the sole competence of the Roman Pontiff, who could, possibly, entrust the Promoter of Justice of the *Congregation for the Doctrine of the Faith* with commencing an investigative process as soon as possible" (McCarrick Report 2020: 286). Pope Benedict appeared to have dragged his red loafers, manufactured by papal shoemaker Adriano Stefanelli, enabling Theodore McCarrick to remain in the public eye until 2011 and beyond. He even managed to travel to Zimbabwe and South Africa in September 2009, as part of a United States Conference of Catholic Bishops' delegation to examine the situation of refugees in the two countries.

On 19 October 2011 Archbishop Carlo Maria Viganò was appointed *Nuncio* to the USA. It appears he did not see this as a promotion. He had hoped to rise within the Secretariat of State with a possible red hat to follow. As the *McCarrick Report* points out, "Viganò, who had been Secretary-General of the Governorate of Vatican City State since 2009 and who believed that he had been promised the position of President of the Governorate, a position normally held by a cardinal, reputedly did not wish to accept Pope Benedict XVI's decision to appoint him as Nuncio to the United States in October 2011, stating that it would undermine his efforts to fight corruption in the Vatican" (*McCarrick Report* 2020: 367 footnote 11200. The *McCarrick Report* makes the following further comment on his appointment, "The written instructions provided to Archbishop Viganò from the *Congregation for Bishops* prior to his arrival at the Nunciature in Washington, D.C., made no mention of McCarrick" (*McCarrick Report* 2020: 367).

For all his shooting off with his mouth, after his fall from grace, Carlo Maria Viganò does not cover himself in glory in the *McCarrick Report*. It states, "Examination of Holy See files revealed no record that Nuncio Viganò ever communicated with Pope Francis about McCarrick in writing, whether before, between or after the June and October 2013 meetings. There is also no other summary or memorandum of the one-on-one meetings between Pope Francis and Viganò. Viganò never reported any interactions with the Pope regarding McCarrick to the Secretariat of State, or to the *Congregation for Bishops*, or to Cardinal Ouellet. He also left no trace of either the June 2013 or the October 2013 meeting with Pope Francis in the files of the Apostolic Nunciature" (*McCarrick Report* 2020: 405–406).

Carlo Maria Viganò's role as the Vicar of Christ's nemesis-in-chief is at first mindboggling. As the *McCarrick Report* notes in a lengthy paragraph, "Although there are no written accounts of the June and October 2013 meetings, several witnesses recalled that Viganò expressed satisfaction with the selection of Francis as Pope during this period, particularly since public reports indicated that Pope Francis intended to address the need for economic and administrative reform for the Vatican City State and the Roman Curia. In an interview, one priest who knew Viganò well stated that, following the June 2013 meeting with Pope Francis, Viganò told him that he and the Pope had discussed reforms, including making reference to a memorandum Viganò had previously prepared regarding such issues. According to this witness, Viganò felt that his meeting with Pope Francis had shown that the Pope seemed convinced about the importance of 'the anti-corruption effort.' The priest stated that 'the way Archbishop Viganò spoke so enthusiastically of the Pope, it sounded like he considered him an ally, so much so that it left me with the impression that he was going to be called back to Rome to help with the reforms'" (*McCarrick Report* 2020: 406).

But another priest's testimony who knew Carlo Maria Viganò well helps to explain his *Volte-face* vis-à-vis the new Pope. "Another priest, who had worked with Viganò for years, likewise stated that he believed that Viganò had nurtured hopes of being recalled by Pope Francis to lead anti-corruption efforts in the Governorate of the Vatican City State. The priest stated, 'He wanted so much to be part of that. He believed deeply that he had real personal contributions to make. He believed that because of his experience he knew more and could help where others could not'" (*McCarrick Report* 2020: 406 footnote 1243).

In his relationship to Theodore McCarrick, Carlo Maria Viganò appears forked tongue. Here is the testimony of the *McCarrick Report*, "On 12 April 2016, Pope Francis accepted Archbishop Viganò's resignation and named Archbishop Christophe Pierre to succeed him as Nuncio in Washington. Viganò and McCarrick continued to exchange letters until Viganò's departure from Washington, mostly with regard to correspondence ultimately destined for the Holy Father or the Holy See. In one letter toward the end of his term as Nuncio, Archbishop Viganò thanked McCarrick 'for your commendable ministry to the Church Universal and your reaching out most recently to China and the Muslim world, efforts that will no doubt bear much fruit.' In June 2016, Archbishop Pierre arrived in Washington as the new Nuncio" (*McCarrick Report* 2020: 427). Archbishop Carlo Maria Viganò was now yesterday's news and as my uncle used to say, his future was firmly behind him.

5. A Velvet Prince of the Catholic Church

Theodore Edgar McCarrick (born July 7, 1930), our villain-in-chief, is an American former cardinal and Archbishop of the Catholic Church. He was Ordained in 1958 — ten years earlier than Carlo Maria Viganò. Less than 20 years later, he became an auxiliary bishop of the Archdiocese of New York in 1977, then became bishop of the Diocese of Metuchen, New Jersey, in 1981. Although an obviously gifted academic with a PhD in Sociology, something of a linguist fluent in English, Spanish and French, some would say Italian and German as well, Theodore McCarrick was something of a late ecclesiastical bloomer being appointed as auxiliary bishop at the advanced age of 47. But once there, his rise was meteoric. From 1986 to 2000, he was the Archbishop of Newark. He was created a cardinal in February 2001 by John Paul II and served as Archbishop of Washington DC from 2001 to 2006. Following allegations of repeated sexual misconduct towards children and seminarians, he was removed from public ministry in June 2018 and became the first cardinal to resign from the College of Cardinals because of claims of sexual abuse in July 2018, and was laicised or defrocked in February 2019, ceasing to be a member of the clergy. Several honours he had been awarded, such as honorary degrees, were rescinded. If ever there was a Lavender *Mafioso* in the Catholic Church in the USA, Theodore Edgar McCarrick was the undisputed godfather. But as John Allen points out, "McCarrick illustrates the risks of clericalism in blinding an entire system to clear warning signs and sincere attempts to blow the whistle"[22] and is the main argument of this article.

6. My Initial Shock upon Reading the Report

My first shock upon reading the *McCarrick Report* was that at the time of his appointment to Washington in 2001 by John Paul II, the following allegations were attracted to Theodore McCarrick like a moth to a light.

a) Priest 1, formerly of the Diocese of Metuchen, claimed that he had observed McCarrick's sexual conduct with another priest in June 1987, and that McCarrick attempted to engage in sexual activity with Priest 1 later that summer;

b) a series of anonymous letters, sent to the National Conference of Catholic Bishops, the Apostolic Nuncio and various cardinals in the United States in 1992 and 1993, accused McCarrick of paedophilia with his "nephews";

c) McCarrick was known to have shared a bed with young adult men in the Bishop's residence in Metuchen and Newark; and

d) McCarrick was known to have shared a bed with adult seminarians at a beach house on the New Jersey shore (McCarrick Report 2020: 67).

This list of allegations raises the question: how did Theodore McCarrick get through the stringent vetting process? The Church is usually a pass master at erring on the side of caution. You can therefore understand my scepticism with the Secretariat of State's disclaimer that "the examination did not reveal evidence that McCarrick's customary gift-giving and donations impacted significant decisions made by the Holy See regarding McCarrick during any period" (*McCarrick Report* 2020: 4) cited above. In the past at least, substantial donations to the Church did not exactly harm one's chances of becoming a *monsignor*. Pope John Paul II allowed Theodore McCarrick to pull the wool over him. He even allowed a letter to his personal secretary to influence his thinking in which Theodore McCarrick lied to the Pope that "In the seventy years of my life, I have never had sexual relations with any person, male or female, young or old, cleric or lay, nor have I ever abused another person or treated them with disrespect" (*McCarrick Report* 2020: 8). This was despite the obvious hyperbole in the letter, a claim not even the Pope could presumably make to the effect "nor have I ever abused another person or treated them with disrespect." I think it would be safe to say that as long you draw breath, even if you are Mother Teresa or Padre Pio, at some point you may have abused another person or at the very least treat them with disrespect. Just recently, the Vice Chancellor of my university upbraided me for calling accountants "bean counters" and I am neither Theodore McCarrick nor John Paul II. All you need to agree with me is to watch the viral video of Pope Francis slapping a woman's hand to free himself at a New Year's Eve gathering to extricate himself from the clutches of an overzealous woman sycophant who got a bit too touchy-feely.[23]

Theodore McCarrick was a sexual abuse snake charmer. A mother interviewed by the *McCarrick Report* tells the following anecdote. "I'm going to tell you a story. There was a day that Ted was over at the house and I was in the kitchen preparing dinner. And I came out of the kitchen and there was Ted sitting on the couch. And he had one son on each side of him and he had a hand on each one of them. On their inner thighs. He was massaging their inner thighs. One hand on the thigh of one and the other hand on the thigh of the other. It was more than strange. It was abnormal. I almost dropped the casserole dish I was holding in my hands. And my husband was sitting directly across from him in a chair and appeared to be oblivious to Ted's behaviour. And when I came to the doorway from the kitchen and I saw what was happening, I nearly fainted. I was shocked and really felt I was going to collapse from what I was witnessing. It was so upsetting. And after Ted left, I said [to my husband], 'We need to get him out of our lives.' [My husband] just refused to understand" (*McCarrick Report* 2020: 39–40).

By the time he was Archbishop in his early 60s, Theodore McCarrick was an incurable but season pro — both sexually and professionally. At one point, in 1992, he was forwarded an anonymous warning letter by the then Cardinal Archbishop of New York, John O'Connor. According to the *McCarrick Report*, he replied wreaking of hubris. "You might want to know that I have shared [the letter] with some of our friends in the FBI to see if we can find out who is writing it. I am afraid he is a sick person and someone who has a lot of hate in his heart" (*McCarrick Report* 2020: 96). In light of the report, we now know who was sick. What Cardinal John O'Connor hoped to achieve by warning a well-known serial sexual abuser is one of the mysteries of an institution in which this was possible. But those of us who have studied clericalism and patriarchy in the Catholic Church are hardly surprised.

Sexual misdemeanours by Theodore McCarrick were known between the Archdiocese of New York, the Nunciature and Rome, yet Theodore McCarrick kept on cropping up in transfers to more high-profile appointments. The *McCarrick Report* notes that "In late June or early July 1999, Pope John Paul II intimated to Cardinal O'Connor that he was considering appointing McCarrick to a different diocese. According to Cardinal O'Connor, 'Our Holy Father seemed to make clear to me in his own subtle way that he was very much interested in and grateful to Archbishop McCarrick, and that he might want to place him in a higher position, even as my successor as Archbishop of New York'" (*McCarrick Report* 2020: 129). At that time Cardinal John O'Connor told Nuncio Gabriel Montalvo that he was aware of "some elements of a moral nature that advised against" consideration of Theodore McCarrick's candidacy for the succession of the Archdiocese of New York (*McCarrick Report* 2020: 129). Wisely, the *Congregation for Bishops* did not transfer Theodore McCarrick by which time he was in his early 70s. In 2000, another prestigious episcopal musical chair was up for grabs: Washington DC and with it a possible red hat. After a lot of to-ing and fro-ing between New York and Rome, Theodore McCarrick was a shoe in. This is how the *McCarrick Report* describes the development. "On 14 October 2000, Archbishop Re arrived at his regular Saturday audience with John Paul II, with the prepared *foglio d'udienza* for the Washington See in hand, and presented it to the Pope. After reviewing the *foglio*, under the printed words '*Ex Audientia Summi Pontificis*' the Pope dated and initialled the document in his own hand: '14.X.2000

JPII.' Below the Pope's initials, Prefect Re handwrote: "The Holy Father nominates as Archbishop of Washington H.E. Msgr. Theodore McCarrick, transferring him from the see of Newark" (*McCarrick Report* 2020: 182). It was an unusual move to say the least, given the reticence of Cardinal John O'Connor who had in the meantime gone to his eternal reward. Meanwhile, Theodore McCarrick was created cardinal by Pope John Paul II at the consistory of 21 February 2001. Surely, Pope John Paul II could not have been oblivious of the mountain of dirty laundry bursting out of the washing baskets belonging to his appointee. In the light of John Paul II's enabling of a paedophile and sexual abuser, Philip Pullella rightly asks, "Saint Pope John Paul II — a hasty halo?"[24] Never mind that in his handling of the Theodore McCarrick sexual abuse scandal, the saintly Pope was blinded by spurious allegations against Polish ecclesiastics. This calls into question the judgement of John Paul II in regard to sexual abuse scandals in general and Theodore McCarrick in particular. Regarding the former, Vanessa Gera of the *Associated Press* reported that "Henryk Gulbinowicz, a prominent Polish cardinal who only days ago was sanctioned by the Vatican over accusations he had sexually abused a seminarian and covered up abuse in another case, has died. He was 97."[25]

Whatever goes up, comes down and soon enough, Theodore McCarrick's scarlet cardinal sins caught up with him. The *McCarrick Report* notes that "In January 2002, the sexual abuse of minors by priests and the handling of such cases by bishops erupted into a major scandal in the United States after the publication of a series of articles in *The Boston Globe*. The intense public scrutiny built steadily through the spring of 2002. The mountain of evidence was overwhelming, leading to his resignation on 22 June 2005, on the eve of his seventy-fifth birthday" (*McCarrick Report* 2020: 215). But on 8 July 2005, Pope Benedict XVI rewarded him with an extension of 2 years beyond the mandatory age of resignation. But the dam of evidence kept on surging. On 16 May 2006, Pope Benedict XVI accepted Theodore McCarrick's resignation as Archbishop of Washington, having revoked the extension. Finally, Theodore McCarrick was off to his troubled retirement. But Theodore McCarrick still managed to keep a high profile.

In 2008, after Pope Benedict XVI's visit to the USA, psychotherapist and former Benedictine monk Richard Sipe published on the Internet a damning "open letter" to Pope Benedict XVI, "Statement for Pope Benedict XVI about the pattern of the Sexual Abuse Crisis in the United States" dated 21 April 2008.[26] According to the author, "sexual aberration" in the Catholic Church was "not generated from the bottom up — that is, only from unsuitable candidates — but from the top down — that is, from the sexual behaviours of superiors, even bishops and cardinals." The author described the problem as "systemic," going on to provide examples, including, he asserted, that of Theodore McCarrick, claiming, "I know the names of at least four priests who have had sexual encounters with Cardinal McCarrick. I have documents and letters that record the first-hand testimony and eye witness accounts of McCarrick, then archbishop of Newark, New Jersey actually having sex with a priest, and at other times subjecting a priest to unwanted sexual advances."[27]

Fast forward, according to the *McCarrick Report*, "On 20 June 2013, Pope Francis received McCarrick briefly at the *Domus Santa Marta*. McCarrick had requested 'five minutes with the

Holy Father' through the Pope's particular secretary on 20 May 2013, and Pope Francis agreed to receive him" (*McCarrick Report* 2020: 402). In the interim, just before Pope Francis dropped the sexual abuse zero-tolerance sledge-hammer on him, Archbishop Giovanni Angelo Becciu, now clipped off all his cardinalate powers but who was then serving as Substitute in the Secretariat of State since his appointment by Benedict XVI in mid-2011, recalled in an interview that he mentioned to Pope Francis the existence of old allegations related to Theodore McCarrick in 2013 and then again at some point between 2014 and 2016. Theodore McCarrick's days were clearly numbered and the writing on the wall. What seems to have been the tipping point, as I have noted above, was a claim of sexual abuse of a minor in 2018. According to the *McCarrick Report*, "On 8 June 2017, the Archdiocese of New York received a claim through its voluntary *Independent Reconciliation and Compensation Program* (IRCP) alleging that McCarrick unlawfully touched Minor 1 during the early 1970s, when the claimant was 16 and 17 years old. This constituted the first accusation against McCarrick of sexual abuse of a minor involving a named victim" (*McCarrick Report* 2020: 433). It was only a matter of when and not if and so, Pope Francis accepted McCarrick's resignation from the College of Cardinals on 28 July 2018. The worst was yet to come.

In detail likely to scandalise the faint-hearted Catholic and perhaps the non-Catholic, the *McCarrick Report* tells us, "On 11 January 2019, and based upon the information gathered during the administrative proceeding, the *Congresso* of the *Congregation for the Doctrine of the Faith* issued a decree finding McCarrick guilty of solicitation during the Sacrament of Confession and sins against the Sixth Commandment with minors and adults, with the aggravating factor of the abuse of power. The *Congresso* imposed on him the penalty of dismissal from the clerical state, after which McCarrick filed a recourse. On 13 February 2019, the Ordinary Session (*Feria IV*) of the *Congregation for the Doctrine of the Faith* considered the recourse presented by McCarrick. The Ordinary Session confirmed the decree of the *Congresso*, and the Holy Father thereafter recognised the definitive nature of the decision" (*McCarrick Report* 2020: 438). In Layman's language he was now defrocked. The unofficial Catholic hierarchy website now lists him simply as "(Layman) Theodore Edgar McCarrick."[28]

The *McCarrick Report* concludes with the words of Pope Francis, straight from the heart, in a personal letter to the people of God written in 2018, "'If one member suffers, all suffer together with it' (1 Cor 12.26). These words of Saint Paul forcefully echo in my heart as I acknowledge once more the suffering endured by many minors due to sexual abuse, the abuse of power and the abuse of conscience perpetrated by a significant number of clerics and consecrated persons. Crimes that inflict deep wounds of pain and powerlessness, primarily among the victims, but also in their family members and in the larger community of believers and nonbelievers alike. Looking back to the past, no effort to beg pardon and to seek to repair the harm done will ever be sufficient. Looking ahead to the future, no effort must be spared to create a culture able to prevent such situations from happening, but also to prevent the possibility of their being covered up and perpetuated. The pain of the victims and their families is also our pain, and so it is urgent that we once more reaffirm our commitment to ensure the protection of minors and of vulnerable adults" (*McCarrick Report* 2020: 449). There in 175 words was Pope Francis' zero-tolerance of sexual abuse, especially of minors, in the Catholic.

7. Five Takeaways from the *McCarrick Report*

There are at least four takeaways from the McCarrick Report: the system of mass manufacture of celibate priests is broken and dysfunctional, an all-male hierarchy and priesthood is no longer fit for purpose, clericalism and patriarchy are part of the problem of much that is wrong in the Church rather than part of the solution and the pyramidal and absolute monarchical model of leadership in the Catholic Church are no longer functional in the postmodern and finally the twin towers of Catholic Church authority and power, secrecy and sovereignty have just been toppled by Pope Francis, an action the Church can ill afford to walk back.

7.1. A Broken and Dysfunctional System Designed to Produce Monsters

People like Theodore McCarrick are attracted to a dysfunctional system. It took 61 years after his ordination for him to get his comeuppance and answer for his cardinal sins of sexual abuse of minors and adults over a career that saw him rise to Cardinal Archbishop of Washington DC. If the selection, accompaniment process leading to his ordination was robust enough, he should have been rooted out and per chance offered help. If there had been a more democratic process of appointing bishops than the one in force, Theodore McCarrick would probably have not made it to the episcopal altar.

7.2. An All-Male and Secretly Appointed Hierarchy is no Longer Fit for Purpose

Celibacy is not the issue here. What is at stake is that a postmodern hierarchy needs to reflect the rest of society. Its leadership and the way of appointment to leadership must be reflective of the rest of society: involving male, female, single, married, straight and gay. A Swiss bishop, Felix Gmür had the following to say about the appointment of bishops. I give my translation first, followed by the German original in square brackets. "Today this procedure is the exception. In the old days it was the norm. It was only with the publication of the ecclesiastical code of canon law (CIC) in 1917 that the right to vote was expressly granted to the Pope. So, the development is only a hundred years old! The fact that in 1917 and in the following years one wanted to create the impression that the papal right of appointment was traditional and that other models of the election of bishops were based on a pure act of grace by the Pope does not change that. That is not right. There have always been different voting procedures. At the beginning of Church history, the broadest possible participation of the faithful and various Church authorities was fundamental. Pope Leo the Great formulated the principle: 'Whoever should preside over everyone must also be elected by everyone'" [*Heute ist dieses Verfahren die Ausnahme. In früheren Zeiten war es die Regel. Erst mit der Herausgabe des kirchlichen Gesetzbuches (CIC) von 1917 wurde das Bischofswahlrecht ausdrücklich dem Papst zugesprochen. Die Entwicklung ist also erst hundert Jahre alt! Daran ändert auch nichts, dass man 1917 und in den Folgejahren den Eindruck erwecken wollte, das päpstliche Ernennungsrecht sei althergebracht und andere Modelle der Bischofswahl beruhten auf einem reinen Gnadenakt des Papstes. Das stimmt so nicht. Es gab schon immer unterschiedliche Wahlverfahren. Grundlegend war zu Beginn der Kirchengeschichte die möglichst breite Mitwirkung der Gläubigen und von verschiedenen kirchlichen Instanzen. Papst Leo der Grossen formulierte den Grundsatz: «Wer allen vorstehen soll, der muss auch von allen gewählt werden»*].[29]

15

7.3. Clericalism and Patriarchy are Part of the Problem in the Catholic Church

Colm Holmes has a stinging critique of both clericalism and patriarchy. He argues that "Change is not happening in the Vatican. Change is happening around the world where lay people and especially women are leading their communities. They are the evangelisers keeping Christ's message of love alive in today's divided world. They are leading liturgies and house Eucharists and ZOOM Eucharists. They understand the Law of Love, where the Vatican clings to the Love of Law. Change is coming from below with the Holy Spirit in the people of God."[30] This vision is a frontal attack on clericalism and patriarchy in the Catholic Church.

7.4. Pyramidal and Absolute Monarchic Leadership in the Catholic Church

For the last two thousand years of Catholicism, a pyramidal and absolute monarchical model of leadership has been promoted and sustained by clericalism and patriarchy. How this is able to survive in the postmodern is the eighth wonder of the world. The one ingredient responsible for this is that the Catholic Church in its western guise is like no other Church. It is both a Church and its headquarters, Vatican City is a country with the Pope as the head of state. With a population of just 1000 people, the Vatican is quite a unique country. This is all thanks to Benito Mussolini and the 1929 Lateran Pact. The city is an absolute monarchy. This means that the reigning monarch has absolute authority, with no restriction of written laws, legislature or customs. Generally speaking, these types of monarchies are hereditary. The Vatican is an elective monarchy by an all-male cohort of one hundred plus cardinals. The Vatican, however, operates as an elective absolute monarchy due to the oath of celibacy Catholic priests take in the pathway to becoming a Pope. Currently, there are only seven absolute monarchies in the world, with most of them operating within the Arabian Peninsula. Of these seven absolute monarchies, the Vatican is the only one which does not rely in any way on hereditary succession. On a smaller or micro level, the absolute authority of the Pope is mirrored in the way bishops are appointed and in the way they lead their dioceses. Such power in the hands of one man does not enhance transparency. Until absolute monarchism is dismantled in the Catholic Church, problems like sexual abuse will continue to fester.

7.5. Vatican Secrecy and Sovereignty Shattered

The fifth and probably most significant takeaway, globally speaking is clearly its historical significance. It shatters two pillars of the Catholic Church's source of power: secrecy and sovereignty. As John Allen rightly points out, "To grasp the full significance of what's happened, let's take a step back. Since 1870, when the Vatican lost its temporal authority and was compelled to become an exclusively spiritual power, operationally it's had two core principles: Secrecy and sovereignty. Secrecy meant we don't air our dirty laundry in public in order to avoid scandal, and sovereignty meant we don't owe an explanation of our actions to anyone. This report doesn't just break with those principles, it shatters them forever."[31] But I very much doubt whether this historic action by Pope Francis will be emulated soon by dioceses across the world.

8. Conclusion

This article has examined a triumvirate of relationships involving Pope Francis, Archbishop Carlo Maria Viganò and Cardinal Theodore McCarrick. The common thread that runs through is how Pope Francis' zero-tolerance of sexual abuse in the Catholic Church was brought to bear on one of the most powerful men of the cloth in the history of the Catholic Church in the United States of America and the role played by the former papal ambassador to the United States, Carlo Maria Viganò. This relationship is played out in a report from the Secretariat of State issued recently, "Report on the Holy See's institutional knowledge and decision-making related to former Cardinal Theodore Edgar McCarrick (1930 To 2017)." The report spares no blushes. Pope John Paul II who promoted Theodore McCarrick through the ranks in spite of sexual abuse allegations and Pope Benedict XVI do not cover themselves in glory. This is unprecedented in a Church document appearing to criticise former Popes, especially given that one of them was still living and a neighbour of the incumbent Pope and the other was fast-tracked to sainthood. All gloves were off. It was the equivalent of an ecclesiastical Ultimate Fighting Championship (UFC). It is all too easy to read the *McCarrick Report* and despair but as a Catholic theologian, there were at least five takeaways staring me in the face: first, to understand men like Theodore McCarrick who sexually abuse others, we have to question the dysfunctional system of mass manufacture of celibate priests which produced them and enabled them. This system that goes back to the Council of Trent (1545–1563) is both broken and dysfunctional. Second, an all-male hierarchy and priesthood that goes back to the Second Lateran Council (1139) is no longer fit for purpose. It needs to be over-hauled. Third, clericalism and patriarchy are part of the problem of much that is wrong in the Catholic Church rather than part of the solution. They make the hierarchy into a self-referential cabal that uses secrecy as its preferred weapon of choice and hard power as the default leadership style rather than soft power. The system needs to be reflective of the rest of society, comprising male, female, married, single, heterosexual and homosexual. Fourth, the pyramid and absolute monarchical model of leadership in the Church is no longer fit for purpose in the postmodern. It is against the servant model of leadership modelled by Jesus Christ. Fifth, the twin pillars of the Catholic Church's authority, secrecy and sovereignty, have now been toppled. May they never be rebuilt.

Finally, the significance of the *McCarrick Report* is nothing short of seismic. As John Allen rightly says, "More basically, think about the precedent this report sets. From now until the end of time, regarding any scandal past or present, if the Vatican refuses to conduct a similar investigation and make the results public, the question always will be: Why not? What are they trying to hide?" And as he adds, "In the end, it's possible the *McCarrick Report* may be remembered as the single most consequential step toward reform during the Francis papacy, not only because of what it reveals about this particular case, but the precedent it sets for how all future cases ought to be handled. Once the genie of transparency is out of the bottle, that is, it's going to be awfully difficult to put it back in."[32]

References

Allen, John L (12 November 2020), "History-making report sets a precedent the Vatican can't walk back," *Crux*, https://cruxnow.com/news-analysis/2020/11/history-making-report-sets-a-precedent-the-vatican-cant-walk-back/ (Accessed on 18.11.2020)

Allen, John L (15 November 2020), "Reality of the abuse scandals now seems A Tale of Two Cardinals," *Crux*, https://cruxnow.com/news-analysis/2020/11/reality-of-the-abuse-scandals-now-seems-a-tale-of-two-cardinals/ (Accessed on 18.11.2020)

Child Rights International Network [CRIN] (2020), "Child sexual abuse in the Catholic Church," https://home.crin.org/issues/sexual-violence/child-sexual-abuse-catholic-church (Accessed on 15.11.2020)

Dockterman, Eliana (26 May 2014), "Pope Declares 'Zero Tolerance' Sex-Abuse Policy," *Time Magazine*, https://time.com/116989/pope-zero-tolerance-sex-abuse-policy/ (Accessed on 17.11.2020)

Gera, Vanessa (16 November 2020), "Gulbinowicz, Polish cardinal accused of abuse, dies at 97," *Associated Press*, https://www.ctvnews.ca/world/gulbinowicz-polish-cardinal-accused-ofabusediesat971.5190775#:~:text=WARSAW%2C%20POLAND%20%2D%2D%20Henryk%20Gulbinowicz,He%20was%2097. (Accessed on 18.11.2020)

Gmür, Felix (2020), "*Aus bischöflicher Sicht: Bischofswahl als geistlicher Prozess*" [From an episcopal point of view: election of a bishop as a spiritual process], *Forum*, https://forum-pfarrblatt.ch/ausgaben/2020/23/bischofswahl-als-geistlicher-prozess/ (Accessed on 16.11.2020)

Holmes, Colm (25 July 2020), "Vatican is living in a Patriarchal Bubble," *Association of Catholic Priests*, https://www.associationofcatholicpriests.ie/2020/07/vatican-is-living-in-a-patriarchal-bubble/ (Accessed on 16.11.2020)

(Layman) Theodore Edgar McCarrick (2020), http://catholic-hierarchy.org/bishop/bmccar.html (Accessed on 16.11.2020

Martin, James (15 December 2017), "It's not about celibacy: Blaming the wrong thing for sexual abuse in the Church," https://www.americamagazine.org/politics-society/2017/12/15/its-not-about-celibacy-blaming-wrong-thing-sexual-abuse-church (Accessed on 16.11.2020)

McCarrick Report (2020), *Report on the Holy See's Institutional Knowledge and Decision-Making Related to Former Cardinal Theodore Edgar McCarrick (1930 to 2017)*, http://www.vatican.va/resources/resources_rapporto-card-mccarrick_20201110_en.pdf (Accessed on 15.11.2020)

Mukuka, Tarcisius (2020), *Anatomy of an Episcopal Dressing Down and Clericalism: A Prince of the Catholic Church and an Ecclesial Irritant*, Munich: GRIN Verlag

O'Malley, Sean (5 December 2013), "Pope Francis sets up Vatican child sex abuse committee," *BBC News*, https://www.bbc.com/news/world-europe-25235724 (Accessed on 15.11.2020)

Papa Francesco (13 March 2013), "Benedizione Apostolica 'Urbi et Orbi' Primo Saluto del Santo Padre Francesco," http://www.vatican.va/content/francesco/it/speeches/2013/march/documents/papa-francesco_20130313_benedizione-urbi-et-orbi.html (Accessed on 15.11.2020)

Pattison, Mark (10 January 2020), "Former cardinal moves from Kansas friary to new location," *National Catholic Reporter*, https://www.ncronline.org/news/justice/former-cardinal-moves-kansas-friary-new-location (Accessed on 18.11.2020)

Pullella, Philip (16 November 2020), "Saint Pope John Paul II — a hasty halo?" *Reuters*, https://www.reuters.com/article/us-pope-johnpaul-sainthood-idUSKBN27W10P (Accessed on 18 November 2020)

Sipe, Richard, "Statement for Pope Benedict XVI about the Pattern of the Sexual Abuse Crisis in the United States," http://www.bishop-accountability.org/news2008/03_04/2008_04_21_Sipe_StatementFor.htm (Accessed on 16.11.2020)

Thoreson, Ryan (21 October 2020), "Pope Francis Supports Same-Sex Civil Unions," *Human Rights Watch*, https://www.hrw.org/news/2020/10/21/pope-francis-supports-same-sex-civil-unions (Accessed on 17.11.2020)

UNICEF (2006), "Child Protection Information Sheet: Child Marriage," https://www.unicef.org/chinese/protection/files/Child_Marriage.pdf (Accessed on 15.11.2020)

Viganò, Carlo Maria (25 August 2018), "Pope Francis covered up McCarrick abuse, former US nuncio testifies (Official Text)," *LifeSite News*, https://www.lifesitenews.com/news/former-us-nuncio-pope-francis-knew-of-mccarricks-misdeeds-repealed-sanction (Accessed on 17.11.2020)

Viganò, Carlo Maria (23 October 2020), "Viganò: The Pope and the Gay Lobby in the Vatican, Intentional Ambiguity," https://www.marcotosatti.com/2020/10/23/vigano-the-pope-and-the-gay-lobby-in-the-vatican-intentional-ambiguity/ (Accessed on 15.11.2020)

Whealin, Julia (2009), "Child Sexual Abuse," *National Centre for PTSD*, https://web.archive.org/web/20090730101002/http://www.ptsd.va.gov/public/pages/child-sexual-abuse.asp (Accessed on 15.11.2020)

Winfield, Nicole (11 November 2020), "Pope Francis vows to end sexual abuse after McCarrick report," https://apnews.com/article/sexual-abuse-by-clergy-sexual-abuse-pope-francis-prayer-17191e15292dff26fae1fe01739d92d1 (accessed on 15.11.2020)

You Tube (31 December 2019), "Indignant Pope Francis slaps woman's hand to free himself at New Year's Eve gathering," https://www.youtube.com/watch?v=3WySwhj2SwE (Accessed on 15.11.2020)

About the Author

 My name is Tarcisius Mukuka. I am a biblical exegete by training. I hail from the Copperbelt where I was born in Luanshya, Zambia. I consider Ndola my hometown where I lived from the age of 2 until I was 19 but I hope to retire back to Luanshya. My ideal job is research in the Humanities and Social Sciences. At undergraduate level, I hold qualifications in Philosophy and Religious Studies (Diploma), Pastoral Theology and Counselling (Graduate Diploma). At graduate level, I hold a Licentiate in Biblical Exegesis from the Pontifical Biblical Institute in Rome Biblical Sciences and at postgraduate level, a doctorate in Biblical Hermeneutics from the University of Surrey in the United Kingdom. My doctoral dissertation was entitled *Orality as Casualty: Contextual and Postcolonial Analysis of Biblical Hermeneutics in Bembaland* (2014). I am currently a senior lecturer in Religious Studies at Kwame Nkrumah University in Kabwe. I am also President of *Theologians against Violence*, a praxis-oriented think-tank with the immediate aim of contributing to free, fair, transparent and peaceful elections in Zambia, beginning with the 2021 General Elections. My research interests include postcolonialism and the Bible, gender and the Bible, the Bible and Misogyny, religion, politics and power. I am the author of *Spoken Voice/Written Word: Negotiating How We Hear/Read the Bible* (2016) published by Lambert Academic Publishing and *In the Eye of a Very Catholic Storm* (forthcoming), by Crown Arts Publishers.

Endnotes

[1] Ryan Thoreson (21 October 2020), "Pope Francis Supports Same-Sex Civil Unions," *Human Rights Watch*, https://www.hrw.org/news/2020/10/21/pope-francis-supports-same-sex-civil-unions (Accessed on 17.11.2020)
[2] *Report on the Holy See's Institutional Knowledge and Decision-Making Related to Former Cardinal Theodore Edgar McCarrick (1930 to 2017)*, http://www.vatican.va/resources/resources_rapporto-card-mccarrick_20201110_en.pdf (Accessed on 15.11.2020)
[3] Carlo Maria Viganò (25 August 2018), "Pope Francis covered up McCarrick abuse, former US nuncio testifies (Official Text)," *LifeSite News*, https://www.lifesitenews.com/news/former-us-nuncio-pope-francis-knew-of-mccarricks-misdeeds-repealed-sanction (Accessed on 17.11.2020)
[4] Eliana Dockterman (26 May 2014), "Pope Declares 'Zero Tolerance' Sex-Abuse Policy," *Time Magazine*, https://time.com/116989/pope-zero-tolerance-sex-abuse-policy/ (Accessed on 17.11.2020)
[5] *Child Rights International Network* [CRIN] (2020), "Child sexual abuse in the Catholic Church," https://home.crin.org/issues/sexual-violence/child-sexual-abuse-catholic-church (Accessed on 15.11.2020)
[6] Bishop Accountability (2020), http://www.bishop-accountability.org/ (Accessed on 22.11.2020)
[7] John L Allen (12 November 2020), "History-making report sets a precedent the Vatican can't walk back," *Crux*, https://cruxnow.com/news-analysis/2020/11/history-making-report-sets-a-precedent-the-vatican-cant-walk-back/ (Accessed on 18.11.2020)
[8] *Association of Rape Crisis Centres in Israel* (ARCCI), (22 November 2020), "What is sexual abuse?" https://www.1202.org.il/en/union/info/what-is-sexual-abuse (22.11.2020)
[9] *UNICEF* (2006), "Child Protection Information Sheet: Child Marriage," https://www.unicef.org/chinese/protection/files/Child_Marriage.pdf (Accessed on 15.11.2020)

[10] Daniel Goleman (24 January 1989), "Sad Legacy of Abuse: The Search for Remedies," *The New York Times*, https://www.nytimes.com/1989/01/24/science/sad-legacy-of-abuse-the-search-for-remedies.html?auth=login-google1tap&login=google1tap (Accessed on 18.11.2020)

[11] Julia Whealin (2009), "Child Sexual Abuse," National Centre for PTSD, https://web.archive.org/web/20090730101002/http://www.ptsd.va.gov/public/pages/child-sexual-abuse.asp (Accessed on 15.11.2020)

[12] James Martin (15 December 2017), "It's not about celibacy: Blaming the wrong thing for sexual abuse in the Church," https://www.americamagazine.org/politics-society/2017/12/15/its-not-about-celibacy-blaming-wrong-thing-sexual-abuse-church (Accessed on 16.11.2020)

[13] Child Rights International Network [CRIN] (2020), "Child sexual abuse in the Catholic Church," https://home.crin.org/issues/sexual-violence/child-sexual-abuse-catholic-church (Accessed on 16.11.2020)

[14] Papa Francesco (13 March 2013), "*Benedizione Apostolica 'Urbi et Orbi' Primo Saluto del Santo Padre Francesco*," http://www.vatican.va/content/francesco/it/speeches/2013/march/documents/papa-francesco_20130313_benedizione-urbi-et-orbi.html (Accessed on 15.11.2020)

[15] *Ibid* — translation from Italian into English mine.

[16] Sean O'Malley (5 December 2013), "Pope Francis sets up Vatican child sex abuse committee," *BBC News*, https://www.bbc.com/news/world-europe-25235724 (Accessed on 15.11.2020)

[17] Nicole Winfield (11 November 2020), "Pope Francis vows to end sexual abuse after McCarrick report," https://apnews.com/article/sexual-abuse-by-clergy-sexual-abuse-pope-francis-prayer-17191e15292dff26fae1fe01739d92d1 (accessed on 15.11.2020)

[18] *Ibid*

[19] Mark Pattison (10 January 2020), "Former cardinal moves from Kansas friary to new location," *National Catholic Reporter*, https://www.ncronline.org/news/justice/former-cardinal-moves-kansas-friary-new-location (Accessed on 18.11.2020)

[20] Carlo Maria Viganò (25 August 2018), "Pope Francis covered up McCarrick abuse, former US nuncio testifies (Official Text)," *LifeSite News*, https://www.lifesitenews.com/news/former-us-nuncio-pope-francis-knew-of-mccarricks-misdeeds-repealed-sanction (Accessed on 17.11.2020)

[21] Carlo Maria Viganò (23 October 2020), "Viganò: The Pope and the Gay Lobby in the Vatican, Intentional Ambiguity," https://www.marcotosatti.com/2020/10/23/vigano-the-pope-and-the-gay-lobby-in-the-vatican-intentional-ambiguity/ (Accessed on 15.11.2020)

[22] John L Allen (15 November 2020), "Reality of the abuse scandals now seems A Tale of Two Cardinals," *Crux*, https://cruxnow.com/news-analysis/2020/11/reality-of-the-abuse-scandals-now-seems-a-tale-of-two-cardinals/ (Accessed on 18.11.2020)

[23] *You Tube* (31 December 2019), "Indignant Pope Francis slaps woman's hand to free himself at New Year's Eve gathering," https://www.youtube.com/watch?v=3WySwhj2SwE (Accessed on 15.11.2020)

[24] Philip Pullella (16 November 2020), "Saint Pope John Paul II — a hasty halo?" *Reuters*, https://www.reuters.com/article/us-pope-johnpaul-sainthood-idUSKBN27W10P (Accessed on 18 November 2020)

[25] Vanessa Gera (16 November 2020), "Gulbinowicz, Polish cardinal accused of abuse, dies at 97," *Associated Press*, https://www.ctvnews.ca/world/gulbinowicz-polish-cardinal-accused-of-abuse-dies-at-971.5190775#:~:text=WARSAW%2C%20POLAND%20%2D%2D%20Henryk%20Gulbinowicz,He%20was%2097. (Accessed on 18.11.2020)

[26] Richard Sipe, "Statement for Pope Benedict XVI about the Pattern of the Sexual Abuse Crisis in the United States," http://www.bishop-accountability.org/news2008/03_04/2008_04_21_Sipe_StatementFor.htm (Accessed on 16.11.2020)

[27] *Ibid*

[28] (Layman) Theodore Edgar McCarrick (2020), Catholic Hierarchy, http://catholic-hierarchy.org/bishop/bmccar.html (Accessed on 16.11.2020)

[29] Felix Gmür (2020), "*Aus bischöflicher Sicht: Bischofswahl als geistlicher Prozess*" [From an episcopal point of view: election of a bishop as a spiritual process], *Forum*, https://forum-pfarrblatt.ch/ausgaben/2020/23/bischofswahl-als-geistlicher-prozess/ (Accessed on 16.11.2020)

[30] Colm Holmes (25 July 2020), "Vatican is living in a Patriarchal Bubble," *Association of Catholic Priests*, https://www.associationofcatholicpriests.ie/2020/07/vatican-is-living-in-a-patriarchal-bubble/ (Accessed on 16.11.2020)

[31] John L Allen (12 November 2020), "History-making report sets a precedent the Vatican can't walk back," *Crux*, https://cruxnow.com/news-analysis/2020/11/history-making-report-sets-a-precedent-the-vatican-cant-walk-back/ (Accessed on 18.11.2020)

[32] *Ibid*